THE ULTIMATE SPY CLUB

MW01538661

SPY TO SPY
SHARING YOUR SECRETS SAFELY

by **Marc Cerasini**

with **Tony and Jonna Mendez**
Consultants

Scholastic Inc.
New York • Toronto • London • Auckland • Sydney
Mexico City • New Delhi • Hong Kong • Buenos Aires

ISBN-13: 978-0-545-01560-8
ISBN-10: 0-545-01560-X
Copyright © 2007 by Scholastic Inc.

Designer: Aruna Goldstein
Illustrations: James W. Elston
Comic Strip Illustrations: Yancey Labat

Photos: Page 19: Graham Stark Photo Library/Hulton Archive/Getty. Page 20: (Napoleon Solo) NBC
Television/Hulton Archive/Getty Images;
(Get Smart) Beltman/Corbis. Page 29: International Spy Museum.

12 11 10 9 8 7 6 5 4 3 2 1   7 8 9 10 11/0

Printed in the U.S.A.

First printing, July 2007

The publisher has made every effort to ensure that the activities in this book are safe
when done as instructed. Children are encouraged to do their spy activities with willing
friends and family members and to respect others' right to privacy. Adults should
provide guidance and supervision whenever the activity requires.

Table of Contents

PSSST!

A spy's job is to gather intelligence or intel—information that's secret and special. Intel is information the enemy does not want you to have!

But it's not enough for a spy to collect information. Once intelligence is gathered, it has to move quickly up the chain of command. That means a spy must be able to pass on the secrets he learned to other friendly agents.

Intelligence is often time sensitive, so quick communication is a must. But fast doesn't mean sloppy! A smart spy knows that espionage is a dangerous game. One of the riskiest jobs of all is agent **commo**.

It is very difficult for spies to communicate secretly. Enemy spies are everywhere, watching and waiting to capture a careless agent. If spies meet face-to-face, they can be observed by the enemy. If they speak, their words can be overheard. Written messages can be intercepted, which is why they are often written in code or invisible ink.

With your latest **Ultimate Spy Club** handbook and spy kit, you'll learn about...

Lost in Translation

A spy must disguise his actions. To become a master spy, you will have to communicate with your fellow agents in secret. To

do this, you must learn to use simple passing techniques, secret codes, and clandestine signals.

Look Who's Talking!

Face-to-face communication is effective but dangerous! When two spies meet— even secretly— there's twice the risk of discovery. Counterspies often pounce at rendezvous points, where they can capture two agents in one trap!

Far Out

Long-range communication lets you communicate with your co-spies without risking being seen together. Signals and codes are often used to transmit information. These messages can be sent in plain sight, right under the enemy's nose.

And more!

Be sure to visit the **Ultimate Spy Club** online at: www.scholastic.com/ultimatespy

This month's secret password is: **secretcommo**

What's in Your *Spy Kit?*

Voice-Recording Card

This voice-recording card is the perfect high-tech tool to pass secret messages. The card has two buttons on the front. Hold down the record button and say your secret message. Once you've passed the card along to a co-spy, he can press the play button and hear the message you recorded. Your fellow agent can record over your message and pass the card back to you for a quick reply.

Keep the card in your wallet, your pocket, or use it as a bookmark. It's perfect for passing secret messages to your friends and fooling your enemies!

MISSION #1:
DISHING UP THE 411

You've just uncovered top secret intelligence that is so hot it's burning a hole in your pocket. What do you do now?

After intelligence is gathered, the information must be passed on quickly and safely. This is the only way it can move up the chain of command. Communication can be personal or impersonal, but which one is better?

In a face-to-face meeting there's less chance of mistakes or confusion. The agents can see and hear each other and ask follow-up questions. But face-to-face encounters are also risky. To avoid detection by counterspies, agents often wear disguises and meet at a **safe site**. Great care must always be taken during a personal meeting, especially when spies are working undercover.

Brief Encounter

When a full length face-to-face meeting isn't possible, spies can still meet to pass information. The brief encounter or **brush pass** is an effective way to trade information without detection.

In a brush pass, two spies meet in a predetermined spot. As they pass one another in the crowd, one agent will slip a package or note into the other's hand or pocket. Sometimes the agents carry the same edition of the newspaper and switch them as they pass.

Sound easy? Don't be fooled. A brush pass must be fast, smooth, and nearly invisible. A master spy knows that it takes practice to master this important skill!

Brush Up On the Brush Pass

Prepare an intel package containing your secret message. This package will be passed by hand to a fellow agent as you "brush past" him on foot. The package

should be small enough to conceal in your hand, but large enough to be grasped easily by your co-spy.

It's important tp practice the brush pass with your co-spy before trying it for real. Make sure to use natural motions with your arms as you pass the package and avoid eye contact with your co-spy. When you walk, don't break your stride.

The pass should be made in one smooth, well-timed move. Both agents' hands should meet in a natural way. The small motion of handing off the package will be masked by the larger movements of your arms and legs. It's tough, but with practice, you'll master this amazing sleight of hand!

When you're ready to try a brush pass for real, be sure to pick a spot that's crowded and where you and your co-spy feel comfortable. Good luck!

SPY TIP:

If you plan on using the voice-recording card to move intel, here are a few tips for a successful brush pass.

The card should be tucked into something you can hold onto easily. A book, magazine, newspaper, or even a small envelope will do.

If you really need to hide your actions from prying eyes, try a disguise. Tuck the library card inside an old book. Now head off to your rendezvous. You'll appear perfectly innocent—like you're on your way home from the local library with the book you just borrowed.

Bag It!

An easier type of brush pass involves two identical packages carried by two different agents. One package contains the secret message; the other is a dummy or fake.

Two spies, each carrying identical shopping bags, briefcases, or pieces of luggage, will meet at a predetermined place. One spy pauses and sets his package on the floor. Another spy approaches and then sets down his bag next to the first one. The first spy will then walk away—after picking up the other spy's package. This is called a bag pass.

The bag pass is almost foolproof and can work in a crowded restaurant, a busy airport, or a bustling train station —anyplace where lots of people gather.

A Sneaky Switch

Give the bag pass a try using a shopping bag, backpack, or even a binder. Sure, the bag pass *looks* easy, but there are several tricks known only to master spies! With practice and a cool attitiude, no one will notice a thing.

When selecting a bag, clever spies choose one with a logo or brand name that's appropriate for the location of the pass. Smart spies want to camouflage their actions, not attract attention.

Make sure both bags are the same size and have roughly the same contents. Don't overstuff the bags or they might look suspicious.

PoP Culture

In the movie **The Firm**, a lawyer uncovers criminal activity inside the law firm where he works. To gather evidence, he uses a pair of identical briefcases to pass secret information to an accomplice inside a busy elevator.

SPY TIP:

For a faster switch, use shopping bags with flat bottoms and looped handles. The flat bottom helps the bag remain upright. The long handles make for easy grabbing. Make sure there are no dangling nametags or visible monograms. Remember, the bags should be identical!

Check the Scene

Choosing a safe and secure location for a brief encounter is as important as the meeting itself. You must constantly be aware of your surroundings.

Before the mission begins, it's wise for you and your co-spies to scout out the location in advance. This is called a **site survey**. During your survey, calculate the amount of foot traffic. Watch people. Notice what they wear. You'll need to blend in with the crowd to make a successful brush pass.

A Better Brush Pass

During your site survey, figure out more than one route in and out of the area. During the actual mission, agents should approach from different directions and arrive promptly. A spy who hangs around waiting to meet an agent who's late can attract unwanted attention!

Clever spies know how to hide their activities in plain sight. A brush pass is best executed while walking in a crowded area. No one will notice the swap, even in a shopping mall, a store, at school, or in the cafeteria.

With practice—and really great timing—you and your co-spy can learn to make a brush pass while rounding a corner. Are you up to the challenge?

In the Bag

A bag pass is easily done in a place where people gather and sit around. A park bench, tables around an outdoor food stand, a crowded restaurant, or a lobby are all great choices.

Sometimes a brief encounter is better performed in a quiet spot, away from prying eyes. A deserted corridor, a stairwell, and a quiet street corner are the perfect places for a clandestine meeting.

But remember, the fewer people around, the more you and your co-spy stand out. It's wise to make a fast switch and get out of the area in a hurry!

The Library Swap

Your voice-recorder looks like a library card. Why not try a brush pass in the library?

One spy can linger at the checkout or information desk and "accidentally" drop his card. The other spy can lean down, pick up the card, and then switch t with a dummy card, which he hands back to the co-spy. The pass is made, and no one is the wiser!

Special Delivery

The most difficult type of brief encounter is called a **moving car delivery**. Master spies often use this method, because it's so fast.

A spy carrying an intel package waits in a dark doorway or behind a bush near a roadway. Another spy approaches in a car. He may stop for a traffic light or simply slow down. The first spy steps out of hiding and drops the package through the car's open window. The driver speeds away and the first spy takes off in the opposite direction. Mission accomplished! The advantages of the moving car delivery are obvious. The pass happens quickly and is followed by a fast getaway. But there are dangers, too!

A moving car delivery only works if there are no other vehicles nearby. It wouldn't do to get stuck in traffic, so a site survey of the encounter zone is a must.

Ready to Roll!

Try a moving car delivery while riding your bike through your neighborhood or in the local park. Remember to be aware of any traffic around you and

choose a place where there are few or no vehicles.

For even more of a challenge, try performing the moving car pass while skateboarding. This takes practice. The master spies out there can try a brush pass while on rollerblades. If you can pull that stunt off, you ought to join the CIA!

The Dead Drop

A **dead drop** is a prearranged place where spies exchange information. This is a hiding place known only to a spy and his fellow agent. A secret message or intel package is left at a dead drop by one spy to be picked up later by his co-spy.

The location of the dead drop is important. In a library, hide your message inside a certain book, and then pass the title along to your co-spy. This method can work with DVD and VHS tape boxes, too.

When concealing your message outside, make sure to hide your intel under something that blends with the environment. Place it under a rock in the park or inside a ball of paper near a trash can. You can also try taping your message behind a sign or under a bench.

MISSION #2:
RECOGNITION SIGNALS

Spies use all sorts of methods to recognize each other without attracting the attention of others. One way is with **recognition signals**.

Sometimes spies will send messages with what they are wearing, what they are carrying, or even where they are standing. A spy might recognize another spy because he's wearing a green sweater, a flag pin, or a particular type of flower worn in a lapel. A female spy might be recognized by her jewelry.

Of course, recognition signals require planning ahead of the mission. Everyone in your spy network must understand each signal so there's no confusion.

Let's say that wearing a white baseball cap means "let's talk." If the co-spy strolling by is being followed, he may tug on his ear or scratch his nose—a signal that it's not safe to approach now. The agent with the hat should back off so as not to blow his cover!

Creating recognition signals is no easy task. But a master spy knows how important this skill is. His life may depend on reading these signals correctly!

POP Culture

In the movie *Twin Peaks: Fire Walk with Me*, two FBI agents get the 411 from a female operative without speaking to her. The woman's message is sent by the color of her dress, the blue rose on her lapel, and the sour expression on her face!

SPY TIP:

Here are a few pointers for picking the right location to send a recognition signal.

➡ Try a busy street corner. On a corner you can be seen from all four directions. This will guarantee your co-spy won't miss you in the crowd.

➡ If possible, get above the herd. Stand on the second or third step in front of a public building. You can even stand on a porch or balcony, as long as your co-spy knows that's where you'll be.

➡ Remember, you're sending a silent signal. You don't have to get close to your co-spy for him to get the message!

➡ After your signal has been sent and received, get out of the area. This is always a smart move, especially after a brush pass or bag switch. And remember, never check the package you get until you are far away from the encounter zone!

Spoken Like a Frenchman

The word **parole** is French for "the spoken word." In spy lingo, a parole is a recognition signal involving a spoken word or phrase. Often a parole is answered with a counterparole—a special coded response. Sometimes paroles and counterparoles can take up an entire conversation!

Paroles are usually bland phrases two strangers might exchange in a short conversation. For example, one spy might open with the phrase, "Warm weather, isn't it?"

His co-spy might reply with a counter-parole like, "You should have been here last week."

This parole might signal that it is safe

to continue the conversation. Or that the timing is bad and the other spy should return in a week. It all depends on the predetermined words and phrases used. Paroles like this can be used on the telephone, or even over the internet as an instant message.

It's important to choose words that sound natural in many countries and cities. Don't use football terms in France, or use a parole that involves a discussion of hamburgers in India. It's wise to choose "universal" topics like the weather.

POP Culture

In *The Pink Panther* movies, Inspector Clouseau always comments on the weather while he checks the room for hidden spies. This is his signal to anyone with him that they shouldn't say anything important.

SPY HISTORY UNCOVERED

During World War II, the British Broadcasting Company broadcasted paroles and recognition signals. These radio messages were coded to inform French Resistance fighters behind the German lines when and where they could expect parachute drops of weapons and supplies.

Advance word about the D-Day invasion at Normandy was also sent to the French freedom fighters using paroles broadcasted over the radio. Secret messages were passed to the French people through paroles spoken in church sermons and written in coded advertisements in newspapers.

You Called?

A short-range agent commo device is a newer, high-tech form of communication used by spies in the field. **SRAC** is electronic communication sent over short distances, usually a mile or less, using special phones.

SRAC is used when the situation is too hot for agents to be seen together. With a SRAC device, spies can still communicate safely. For example, two spies could enter a city park from opposite directions. They could exchange an electronic radio transmission in a few seconds.

Short-range agent commo devices use coded bursts that are difficult to intercept and impossible to trace. No one can find a spy's location by following the signal, as you can with a conventional cell phone. Cell phone transmissions are not coded, either, so it is possible to intercept conversations as well as trace them.

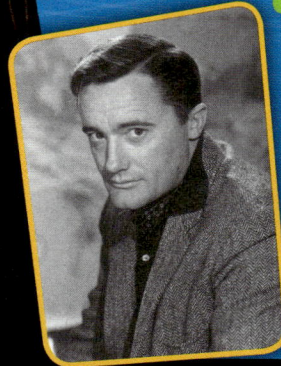

Don't you wish you and your friends had SRAC phones? Unfortunately, SRAC devices cost a lot of money to develop. Even worse, if the enemy cracks your code (or an enemy spy steals it from you!), technicians have to start from scratch to come up with a brand new system.

Try communicating with your co-spies using walkie-talkies. You can make your communication more secure by using coded phrases, or even Morse code, to send your secret information.

POP Culture

Agent Maxwell Smart on *Get Smart* had a communications device that did double duty—as a shoe! Like those men from U.N.C.L.E., Smart's shoe phone was short range. Perhaps it's just too expensive to make a "sole" call!

SPY TIP:

You can't have an SRAC (hey, dude—they're classified!), but you can try something almost as good. Use the instant messaging system on your computer.

The short-hand phrases used by many IM users is almost like a code. LOL if you want to, but it makes sense.

If you want to disguise your own communication, work out code phrases with your co-spies. That way, even if the enemy is looking over your shoulder, he'll be clueless!

MISSION #3:
THE IMPERSONAL TOUCH

Espionage has been around as long as nations have competed against one another for power. Since the beginning, spies have been hiding secret messages under rocks or in hollow trees for another spy to find.

Any kind of commo where spies avoid real-time contact is called **impersonal communication**. Impersonal commo is generally more secure than personal contact for a lot of reasons.

In dangerous situations, personal contact should be avoided. Everyone is watching each other and the authorities are watching everyone. A spy may be put under surveillance and not know it. If he were to meet a fellow agent face-to-face, that spy and the operation itself could be exposed. Both agents could be captured—or worse!

To stay safe and secure, master spies have invented interesting kinds of impersonal commo. That's why knowing how to make a good dead drop is so important.

SPY HISTORY uNcovEred

From 1979 to 2001, Robert Hanssen stashed thousands of secret documents at a dead drop under a bridge outside Washington, D.C., for Russian agents to pick up.

Hanssen's concealment device was simple. He stuffed his secret messages inside a plastic garbage bag. Because it was dark under the bridge, the black bag was waterproof and practically invisible!

REAL SPY GADGETS

When secret messages are left at a dead drop for another agent to pick up, often a concealment device is used. These ingenious devices help spies hide their secret messages from the enemy.

Cans filled with coffee or shaving cream have been used by master spies of the past. These devices are often built with secret compartments hidden behind screw-off bottoms. Hollowed-out books also come in handy. Secret messages are placed inside these items and passed on to other agents.

False teeth and artificial eyes have been used to smuggle microfilm and microdots. Russian spies operating in New York City in the 1950s used a hollow nickel to pass information. Other disguised intel packages include fake rocks, matchbooks, gum wrappers, and hollow coins.

Secret Writing

Secret writing is probably the oldest form of impersonal commo. Technology has improved since the days of parchment and wax tablets, but secret writing is still a simple and effective means of communication.

Secret writing is done with secret inks and secret developers. Sounds like you need a chemist or James Bond's gadget-man Q, right? Believe it or not, you don't! In fact, you can make many of the secret inks yourself, from common household items.

Did Life Hand You Lemons?

Believe it or not, you can use lemon juice to make good invisible ink. Just squeeze and strain. To write, use a wooden toothpick or a Q-tip as a pen.

Dip your pen into the juice and write on a blank piece of paper using block letters. You might need a desk lamp—writing invisibly takes some getting used to! When the letter is done, let the ink dry before handling.

To make the ink visible you just apply heat to the letter. Hold the secret letter up to a lamp, or have an adult use steam from a tea kettle or iron to heat it up. Then the hidden words will appear!

All out of lemons? Try milk!

Grape Idea!

Another ink used by master spies is made by dissolving one teaspoon of bicarbonate of soda in a cup of water. Use the toothpick method to write. Make the letters appear by using purple grape juice applied with Q-Tips.

Go Postal!

Send a secret message in a **cover letter** to a co-spy trained to develop invisible ink. Choose an innocent subject like your camping trip or summer vacation. Leave enough space between each line to write your secret message with invisible ink. When the cover letter is completed,

write the secret message between the visible lines.

Make sure you've let your fellow agent know to expect a secret message. Use a code to mark the cover letter on the outside of the envelope like a smiley face or scribbled star on the back.

Are You "Cutout" to Be a Spy?

For secure communication, master spies will use an **accommodation address** when sending cover letters. Sometimes an accommodation address is a fake business. Sometimes it's a real home, with people living there. They may not even know about the secret message. Sometimes these people are asked to forward cover mail to another address where the spy receives it.

If intelligence is delivered by messenger, that messenger is called a **cutout**. A cutout knows nothing about the spying. He's only hired to deliver the message to an undercover agent. You can use an unsuspecting friend as a

cutout. Simply ask them to deliver a letter containing a secret message to a co-spy!

Spies will also hide intel at a dead drop where another spy will find it. They use concealment devices that blend in with the environment to help hide the intel from the enemy.

SPY TIP:

If you're going to leave intel at a dead drop, it's important to create the right intel package. If the package is going to lay around for a while, use a weatherproof concealment device.

You can also try a bike toss with your dead drop. An effective delivery device is a rolled up newspaper. Nothing flies so true as a well-tossed, folded newspaper. But a paper isn't weatherproof, so prompt pickup is important.

Conduct a site survey beforehand. Scope out the routes and the foot and vehicle traffic.

REAL SPY GADGETS

Microdots were invented about the same time as the first photographs in the 19th century. They are still one of the most secure forms of agent commo and are used in espionage operations today.

Microdots are photographs tiny enough to be hidden in a period at the end of this sentence. (Yeah, that one!)

If you don't know the exact location of a microdot hidden in a book, chances are you will never find it.

A trained spy can make a microdot with an ordinary camera. Microdots can be read with a small Stanhope "bullet" lens the size of a grain of rice. In a pinch, a trained agent can read a microdot with an ordinary camera or a microscope.

Microdots can be hidden in letters sent through the mail, in a magazine, or even a post card. There's also a way to make digital microdots and send them over the internet.

Signs of the Times

Signs and signals are other great ways to send messages without the risk of personal contact. A signal might be something simple, like a chalk mark on a mail box, telephone pole, or curb.

The mark might signal you are ready to make a dead drop. Another agent sees the mark from a distance, yet no one else knows a message has even been sent.

Different chalk marks can be used. A straight line may mean "I'm ready to pick up a drop."

An "X" may signal danger: "I'm being followed."

The most famous signal in United States history was when Paul Revere checked the lights of Old North Church. "One if by land, two if by sea!" was the secret signal that revealed the movements of the enemy. When the signal went up, Paul Revere made his

famous ride to warn the countryside that "The British are coming!"

Codes and Spy Radios

An old form of long range agent commo is the one way voice link. An OWVL is practically impossible to trace. There is no way to know who is receiving the message over their short-wave receiver. The broadcast is made by a powerful transmitter strong enough to be heard around the world.

An OWVL coded message is often sent in groups of five numbers. These numbers are decoded with a one-time pad (OTP), which has the precise page that contains the cipher.

No one without that exact page of the OTP can understand the message. When another message is sent later, another page of the one-time pad is used, this one containing a new and different code cipher. This "one-time" use of each page gives the OTP its name!

Pop Culture

The movie *Enigma* is set in World War II. It tells the amazing story of the Nazi code machine called Enigma and the brilliant men and women who cracked it. The Germans used Enigma to direct the activities of their submarines in the North Atlantic. It produced a code that was almost impossible to crack. The movie is set at Bletchley Park, a real school in England that turned scientists and mathematicians into master spies.

Listen Up!

You can listen to real spies communicate right now—if you know where to tune in.

If you have a simple short-wave radio, tune into 86855 kHz or 8010 on the hour. You might hear a female voice repeating strings of numbers in a Spanish monotone. This is Cuban intelligence broadcasting coded instructions from Havana to spies inside the USA.

Or you can tune into 11545 kHz and you might hear a few notes from an English folk song. This tune is followed by a voice repeating strings of numbers. That's British MI6 broadcasting from Cyprus.

On 6840 kHz you might hear another voice repeating letters. This is station "E10" which broadcasts messages to Israel's Mossad spies.

Needless to say, US intelligence agencies monitor these broadcasts. There are spies are all around you, so remember to keep your eyes peeled and your ears open!

Mission
ACCOMPLISHED!

In the modern age of dead drops, secret writing, cell phones, and instant messages, agent commo is a little bit easier—and a whole lot more risky. When sending the 411 or using your voice recorder, remember the tips you've learned here!

MARC CERASINI
Writer

When not writing for kids, Marc publishes thriller novels and books about advanced military hardware and technology. He lives a furtive, undercover existence in New York City.

TONY AND JONNA MENDEZ
Consultants

Tony and Jonna spent their careers at the CIA. They worked overseas protecting American spies and the foreign assets working for the U.S. government. They were specialists in disguise and documents. Tony Mendez was named one of the CIA's top spies in the last 50 years.

Glossary

Here are some spy terms that you need to know.

Accomodation Address – An address used to allow spies to mail materials securely

Bag Pass – The exchange of materials using two identical bags

Brush Pass – The quick passing of a message from one agent to another as they stroll past one another

Commo – Spy slang for "communication"

Concealment Device – An object used to hide or carry secret messages

Cover Letter – An innocent-looking letter used to cover up a hidden message

Cutout – An unsuspecting messenger who unknowingly delivers secret communication between spies

Dead Drop – A temporary hiding place used for secret communications between co-spies

Impersonal Communication – Any commo between spies that does not involve face-to-face contact.

Microdot – A tiny photograph containing a message or data

Moving Car Delivery – A method of exchanging materials in which one spy delivers a package to a car as it passes by

Parole – A spoken recognition signal that allows two spies to identify each other as friendly agents

Recognition Signal – A sign used to identify a spy or secretly communicate a message

Safe Site – A place that is unknown to the enemy and safe for spies to meet

Secret Writing – Technique used to hide messages

Site Survey – The scouting of an area before an actual meeting to determine the safest way to accomplish a mission

SRAC – Short-Range Agent Contact. When agents interact and exchange information by coming into close contact with one another.